CAMBRIDGE
Primary English

Phonics Workbook B
Gill Budgell & Kate Ruttle

My name is ……………………………………………………

I am ……………………………………………… years old.

I go to ……………………………………………………..

……………………………………………………. School.

CAMBRIDGE
UNIVERSITY PRESS

University Printing House, Cambridge CB2 8BS, United Kingdom

One Liberty Plaza, 20th Floor, New York, NY 10006, USA

477 Williamstown Road, Port Melbourne, VIC 3207, Australia

314–321, 3rd Floor, Plot 3, Splendor Forum, Jasola District Centre,
New Delhi – 110025, India

103 Penang Road, #05 – 06/07, Visioncrest Commercial, Singapore 238467

Cambridge University Press is part of the University of Cambridge.

It furthers the University's mission by disseminating knowledge in the pursuit of education, learning and research at the highest international levels of excellence.

www.cambridge.org Information on this title: www.cambridge.org/9781108789967

© Cambridge University Press 2021

This publication is in copyright. Subject to statutory exception
and to the provisions of relevant collective licensing agreements,
no reproduction of any part may take place without the written
permission of Cambridge University Press.

First published 2015
Second edition 2021

20 19 18 17 16 15 14 13 12 11 10 9 8 7 6 5 4 3 2 1

Printed in Malaysia by Vivar Printing

A catalogue record for this publication is available from the British Library

ISBN 978-1-108-78996-7 Paperback with digital access (1 Year)

Cambridge University Press has no responsibility for the persistence or accuracy of URLs for external or third-party internet websites referred to in this publication, and does not guarantee that any content on such websites is, or will remain, accurate or appropriate. Information regarding prices, travel timetables, and other factual information given in this work is correct at the time of first printing but Cambridge University Press does not guarantee the accuracy of such information thereafter.

....

NOTICE TO TEACHERS IN THE UK
It is illegal to reproduce any part of this work in material form (including photocopying and electronic storage) except under the following circumstances:
(i) where you are abiding by a licence granted to your school or institution by the Copyright Licensing Agency;
(ii) where no such licence exists, or where you wish to exceed the terms of a licence, and you have gained the written permission of Cambridge University Press;
(iii) where you are allowed to reproduce without permission under the provisions of Chapter 3 of the Copyright, Designs and Patents Act 1988, which covers, for example, the reproduction of short passages within certain types of educational anthology and reproduction for the purposes of setting examination questions.

Cover image by Pablo Gallego (Beehive Illustration)
Image on p.11: Magnilion/Getty Images.

Contents

Page	Letters and sounds Example words are given where there are alternative pronunciations.	Templates
4–5	sh, th (thin, this), ch, ng, nk	6, 4
6–7	ai, ee, ie, oa, oo (book), oo (moon)	4, 3
8–9	oi, ow (cow), ar, or, ir, er (farm<u>er</u>)	2
10–11	ai, a_e, ay	5
12–13	ee, ea (eat), e	1
14–15	ie, i_e, igh, y (fly)	6
16–17	oa, o_e, ow (slow), oe	4
18–19	oo (moon), u_e, ue, ew and oo (book), u (put)	5
20–21	ar, ir, ur, or, aw, ore	2
22–23	ow (now), ou (house); oi, oy	1
24–25	**air**, are (share), **ear** (near), eer	6
26–27	**f**, ff, ph; **w**, wh	4
28–29	Look back	3
30–31	**a** (apple, apron, plant, swan); **e** (egg, me, basket)	2, 1
32–33	**i** (tick, pie); **y** (yak, baby)	2
34–35	**o** (hot, colour, most); **u** (hut, bush, glue)	4
36–37	**ie** (tie, field); **ea** (bead, bread)	5
38–39	**ow** (owl, elbow); **ou** (house, you)	2, 3
40–41	**c** (cat, city); **g** (girl, giraffe)	4
42–43	Look back	3
44–45	'**s**': seven; '**z**': trees	1
46–47	'**sh**': sta<u>ti</u>on; '**zh**': mea<u>s</u>ure; '**ch**': pic<u>t</u>ure; '**j**': bridge	6, 5
48–49	More about '**ai**', '**ee**', '**ie**', '**oa**'	4
50–51	More about '**oo**', '**or**', '**ir**', '**ar**'	6
52–53	'**er**': fath<u>er</u>, zebr<u>a</u>, visit<u>or</u>	2
54–55	Look back	3
56–63	Teaching phonics using Phonics Workbook B	
64	Pronunciation guide	

Template 6 and 4

Trace the letters and say the sounds.

sh th ch ng nk

Say and write the words.

ship

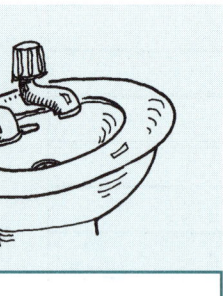

Draw and write a word ending with **sh**.

Draw and write a word beginning with **ch**.

4

sh, th, ch, ng, nk

Choose the correct words to finish the sentences.

The _____ is cross. He has a mark on his _____ .

sing
king
wing

chin
chip
shin

Thin
Them
This

" _____ is not good."

"Rub it _____ a _____ ."

this
with
them

chip
chick
cloth

To read this word, say c-l-o-th

Rich
Much
Such

" _____ a lot of fuss!"

Think
Thank
Thick

" _____ you."

5

Template 4 and 3

Trace the letters and say the sounds.

Say these as a short sound like **book**.

ai ee ie oa oo oo

Say these as a long sound like **moon**.

Use the pictures. Say the words.
Write one letter in each box.

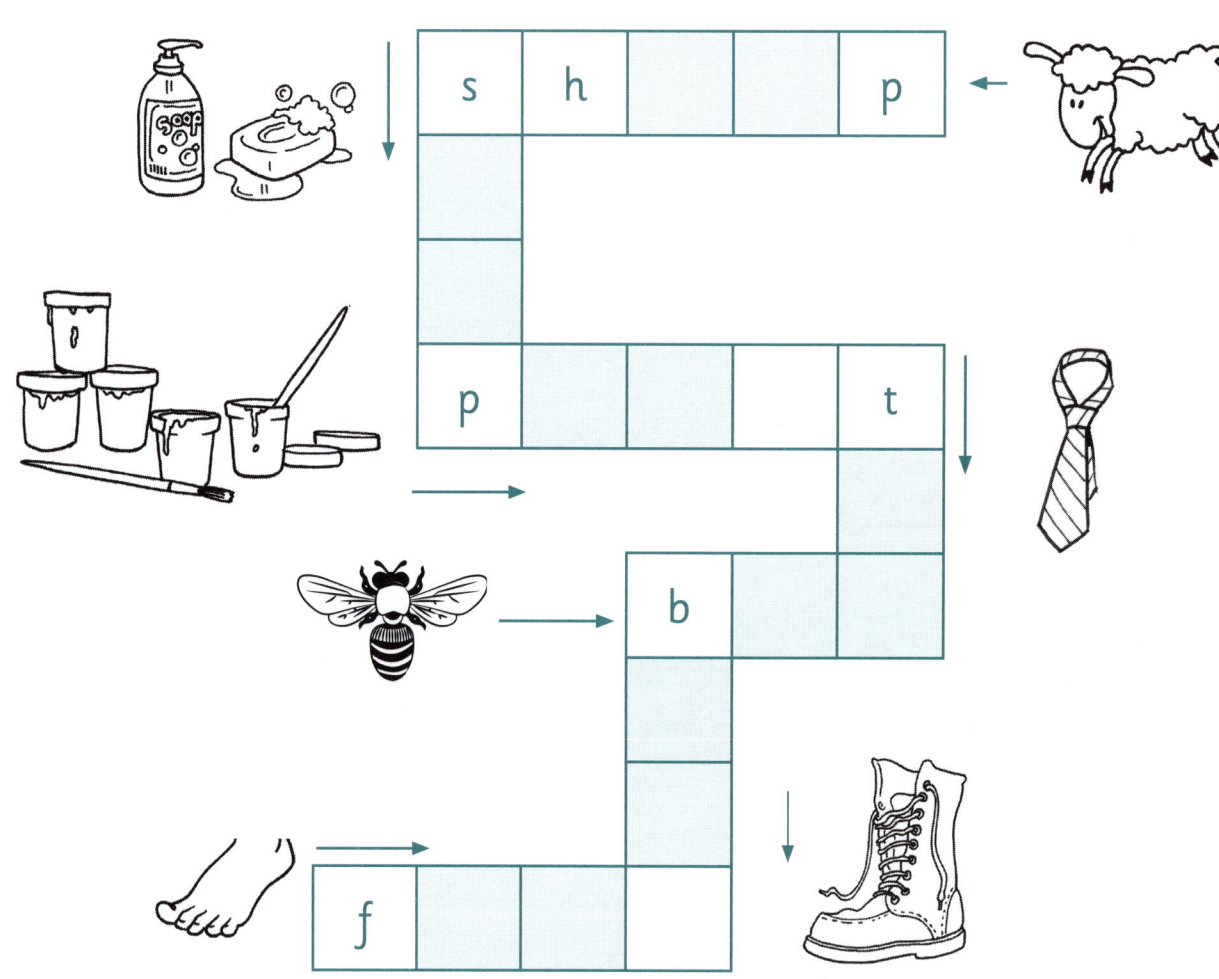

Write the words again.

ai _____ oa _____

ee _____ oo (short) _____

ie _____ oo (long) _____

ai, ee, ie, oa, oo, oo

Read the questions. Write **yes** or **no**.

Is the sheep in the road? _____

Can the big man get his foot in the boot? _____

Is her food on a fork? _____

Can they sail a boat? _____

Template 2

Trace the letters and say the sounds.

oi ow ar or ir er

Say the words. Draw lines to join each word to the correct picture.

fork
jar
bird
cow
oil
crown
girl
flower

oi, ow, ar, or, ir, er

Say the words. Choose the correct letters to finish the words.

sh ___ k	sh ___ t	___ l
st ___	c ___ n	___ m
sk ___ t	c ___	h ___ n

9

Template 5

Trace the letters and say the sounds.   A line between letters shows where a letter is missing.

ai   a_e   ay

Read the story. Underline the words with **ai**, **a_e** or **ay**.

Layla came for a play day.

She came to play games with me.

First, we had a race.

Then we went sailing in the rain.

Then we made cakes with Mum.
We had a good play day.

Write two of the words in each box.

Words with **ai**	Words with **a_e**	Words with **ay**

10

ai, a_e, ay

The robot turns mixed-up letters into words. Finish the words.

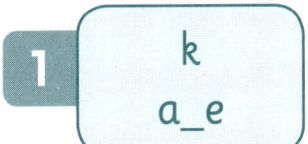
1. k a_e

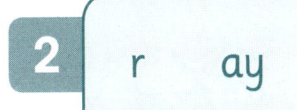
2. r ay

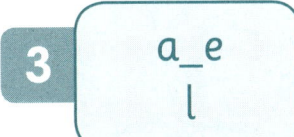
3. a_e l

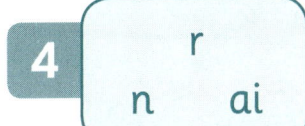
4. r n ai

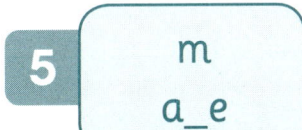
5. m a_e

6. a i l

1. bake

2. t _____

3. t _____

4. t _____

5. c _____

6. t _____

Read and trace the words.

came   made   make
today   always

11

Template 1

Trace the letters and say the sounds.

ee ee ee ea ea ea

Draw lines to join each word to the correct picture.

meal   reading   cheese   tree   feet   bee

Sort and write the words in the correct boxes.

ee	ea

12

ee, ea, e

Write **ee** or **ea** next to the pictures.

ee ee ee ea ea ea

Read and trace the words.

please

people

Read the sentence.

Please give these sweets to the people.

Template 6

Trace the letters and say the sounds.

ie   i_e   igh   y

Read the words and draw the pictures.

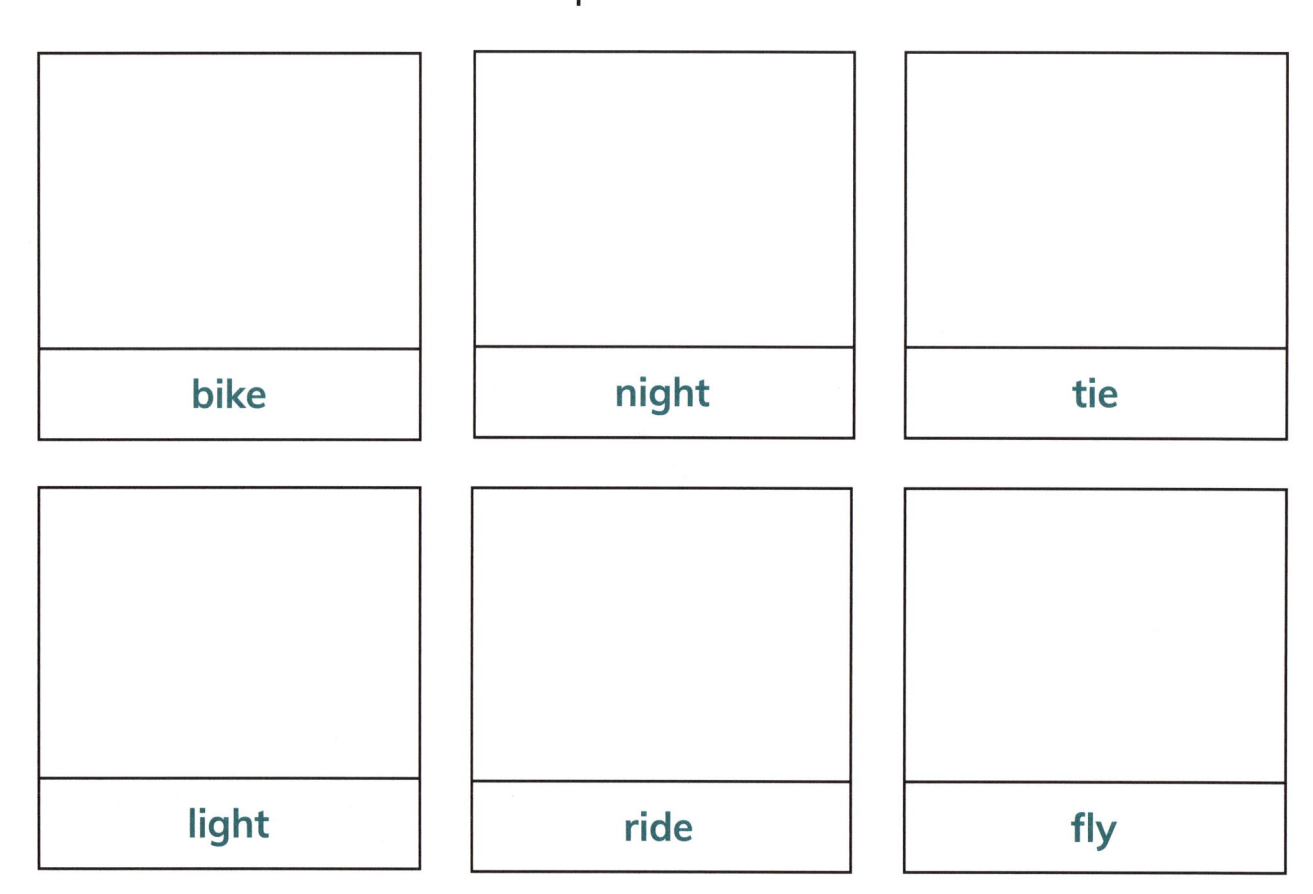

bike	night	tie
light	ride	fly

Write the words in the correct boxes.

ie	i_e	igh	y

ie, i_e, igh, y

Read and trace the words.

by　　my　　like

time　　night

Choose the correct words to finish the sentences.

It is _____ for bed.

Please can you read _____ book?

I _____ it when you are asleep _____ nine o'clock.

Now go to sleep. Good _____.

15

Template 4

Trace the letters and say the sounds.

Say this like the sound in **slow**.

oa   o_e   ow   oe

Use the pictures. Say the words.
Write one letter in each box.

Write the words in the correct boxes.

oa	o_e	oe	ow

16

oa, o_e, ow, oe

Trace the letters and say the sounds.

oa   o_e   ow   oe

Say the words. Choose the correct letters to finish the words.

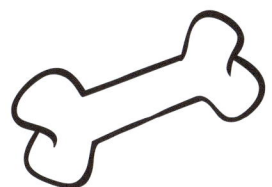

oa
o_e

b _____

o_e
oa

c _____

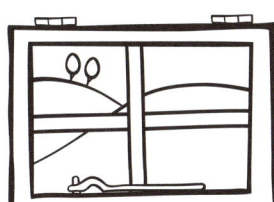

oe
ow

win _____

oe
ow

_____

Read the black words.
Circle the coloured words that match the black words.

don't   do   dont   don't   dont'   don't

old   do   old   low   don't   old   do   old

so   do   to   so   go   so   of   so   no   so

Template 5

Trace the letters and say the sounds.

oo   ue   u_e   ew ← Long sounds

Short sounds → oo   u

Read the story. Underline the words with **oo, ue, u_e, ew, oo** or **u**.

I had a good dream …
I put on my new blue boots.

I grew wings and I flew up to the moon.
I played tunes on a flute.

Then my wings came off and
I fell into a bush. I stood up and
shook myself … and then I woke up.

Write three words with a long **oo** sound.	Write three words with a short **oo** sound.
oo, ue, u_e, ew	oo, u

18

oo, ue, u_e, ew and oo, u

The robot turns mixed-up letters into words. Write the words.

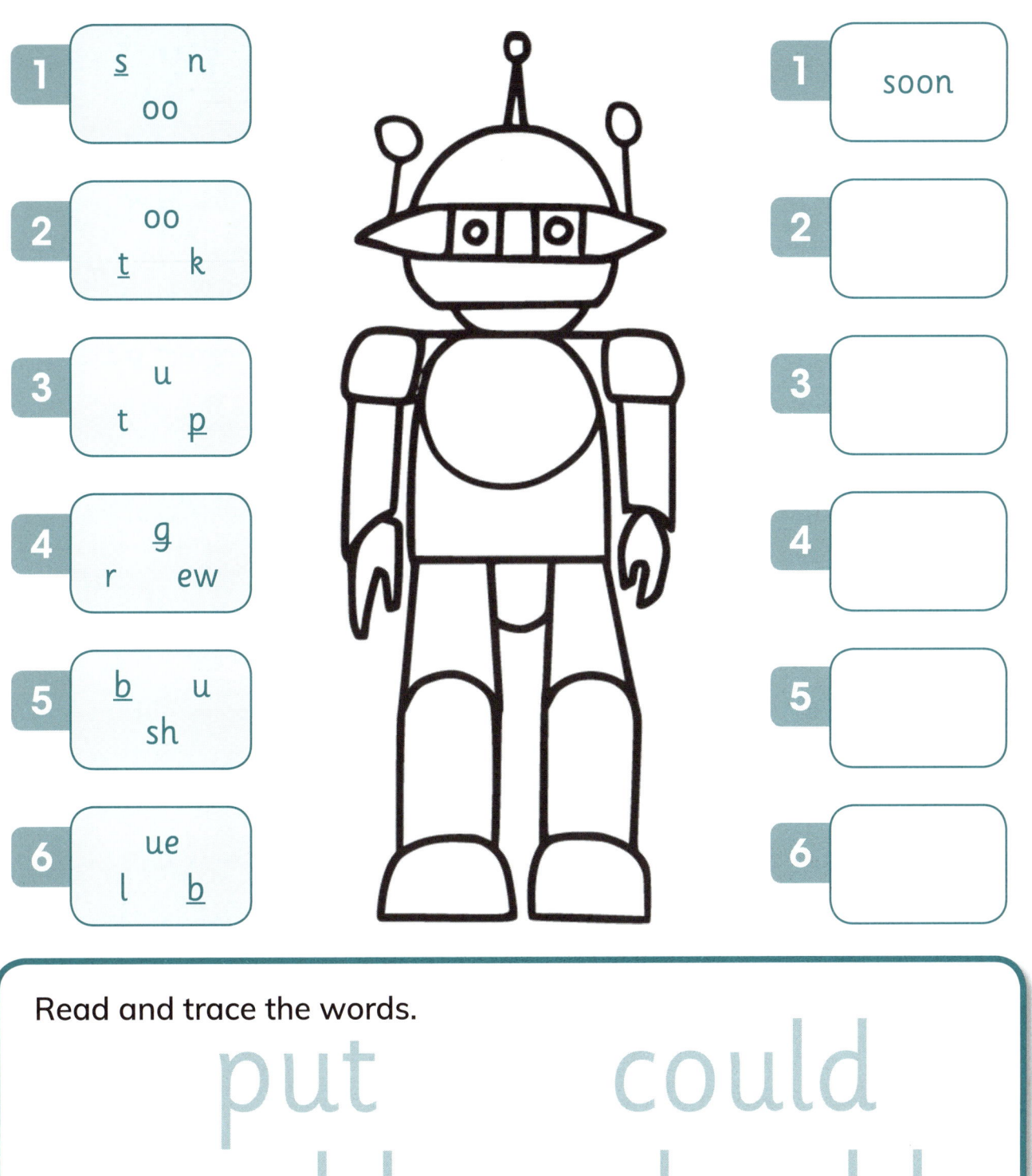

1. s n oo — soon
2. oo t k
3. u t p
4. g r ew
5. b u sh
6. ue l b

Read and trace the words.

put   could
would   should

19

Template 2

Trace the letters and say the sounds.

ar   ir   ur

or   aw   ore

Say the words. Draw lines to match each word to the correct picture.

ar, ir, ur, or, aw, ore

Say the words. Choose the correct letters to finish the words.

g ____ l   sn ____   sh ____ k

h ____ t   s ____   f ____ k

Read and trace the words.

are   **your**

saw   **more**

Choose the correct words to finish the sentences.

I s_____ y_____ book about the moon and the stars.

There a_____ m_____ stars tonight. Shall we look at them?

Template 1

Trace the letters and say the sounds.

Say this like the sound in **now**.

Draw lines to join each word to the correct picture.

owl

mouse

cloud

shout

boy

coin

soil

enjoy

Sort and write the words in the correct boxes.

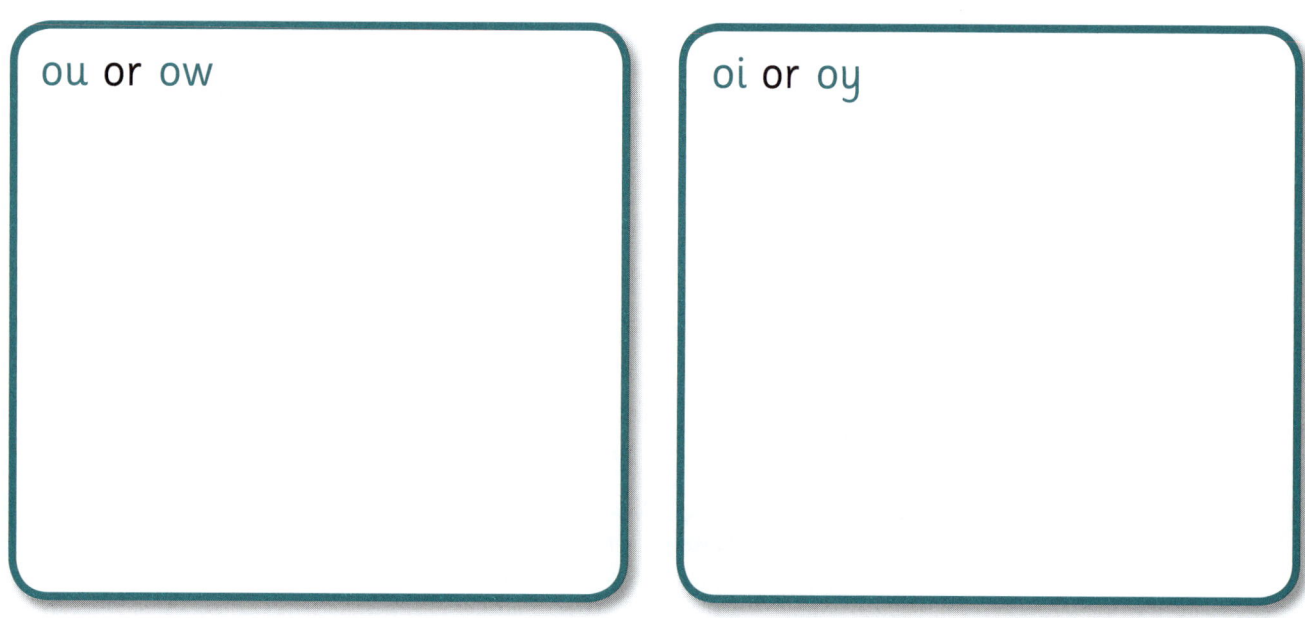

ou or ow

oi or oy

ow, ou, oi, oy

Trace the letters and say the sounds.

ow   ou   oi   oy

Draw lines to join each spelling to the correct picture.

Sound out **a-b-ou-t**

Read and trace the word.

about

Sound out **e-n-j-oy**

Read and trace the word.

enjoy

Read the sentence.

We are about to enjoy our meal.

Template 6

Trace the letters and say the sounds.

air   are ← Say this sound like the sound in **share**.

Say this like the sound in **near**. → ear   eer

Read the words and draw the pictures.

| chair | stare | hair |

| ear | deer | cheer |

air, are, ear, eer

Read and trace the words.

there

their

dear

deer

Choose the correct words to finish the sentences.

_____ Grandpa.

We are camping.

_____ are _____ near our tent.

_____ ears are brown and they have big antlers.

It is funny when they stand and stare at us!

From Afia.

Template 4

Trace the letters and say the sounds.

ff   ph   w   wh

Use the pictures. Say the words. Write one letter in each box.

Circle the pairs of letters that make one sound.

f, ff, ph, **w**, wh

Trace the letters and say the sounds.

f ff ph w wh

Say the words. Choose the correct letters to finish the words.

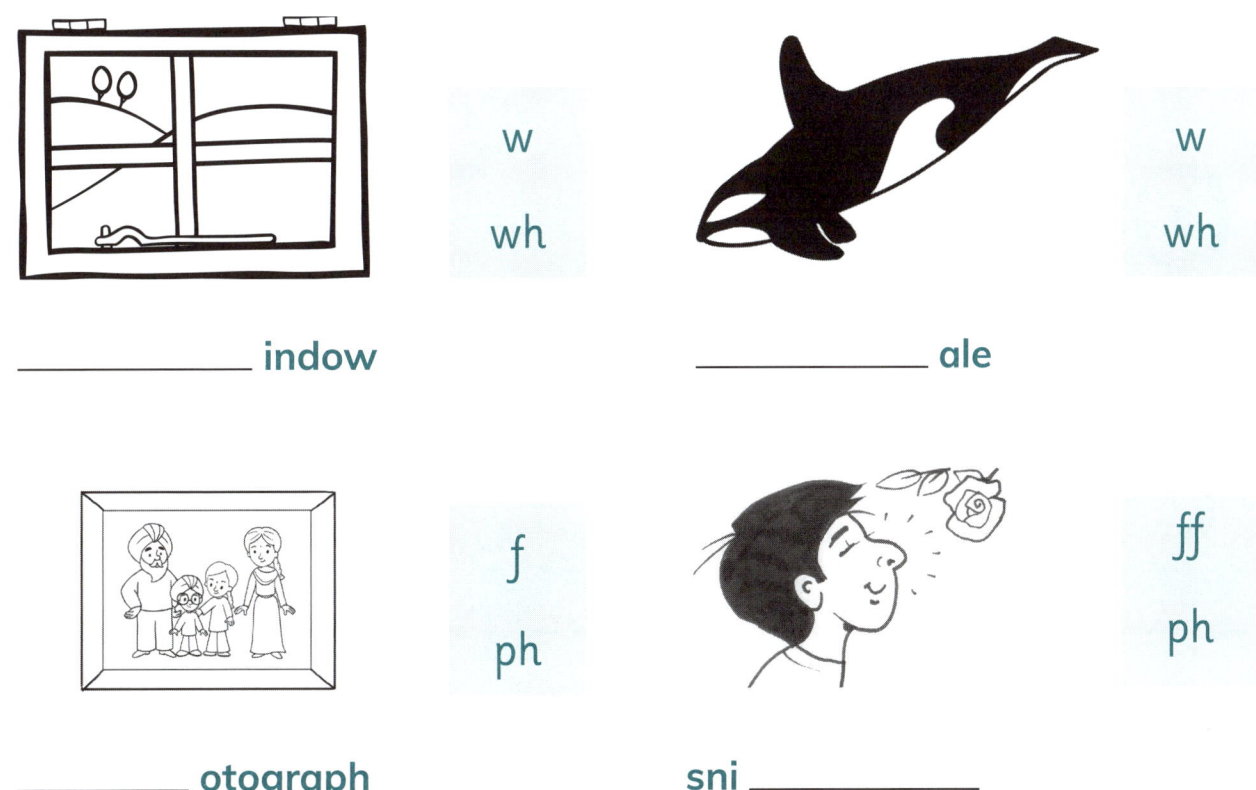

_____ indow   w / wh

_____ ale   w / wh

_____ otograph   f / ph

sni _____   ff / ph

Read the black words.
Circle the coloured words that match the black words.

where   there   where   were   where

when   then   when   them   when   when

Template 3

> Look back

Check what you know!

Write the words.

Look back

Read and trace the words.

some   one

Read the questions. Write **yes** or **no**.

 Is her new coat white? _____

 Is he cutting some wood with a hammer? _____

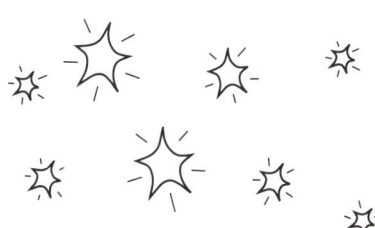 Do stars shine at night? _____

 If I glue these bits, will I make a boat? _____

29

Template 1 and 2

We can say letter **a** in different ways so it sounds like: 'a', 'ay', 'o' or 'ar'.

Say the words. Draw lines to join the words where letter **a** sounds the same.

Sort and write the words in the correct boxes.

'a' sound as in ant	'ar' sound as in class	'ay' sound as in day	'o' sound as in was

a and e

We can say letter **e** in different ways so it sounds like: 'e', 'ee' or 'i'.

Say the words. Draw lines to join the words where letter **e** sounds the same.

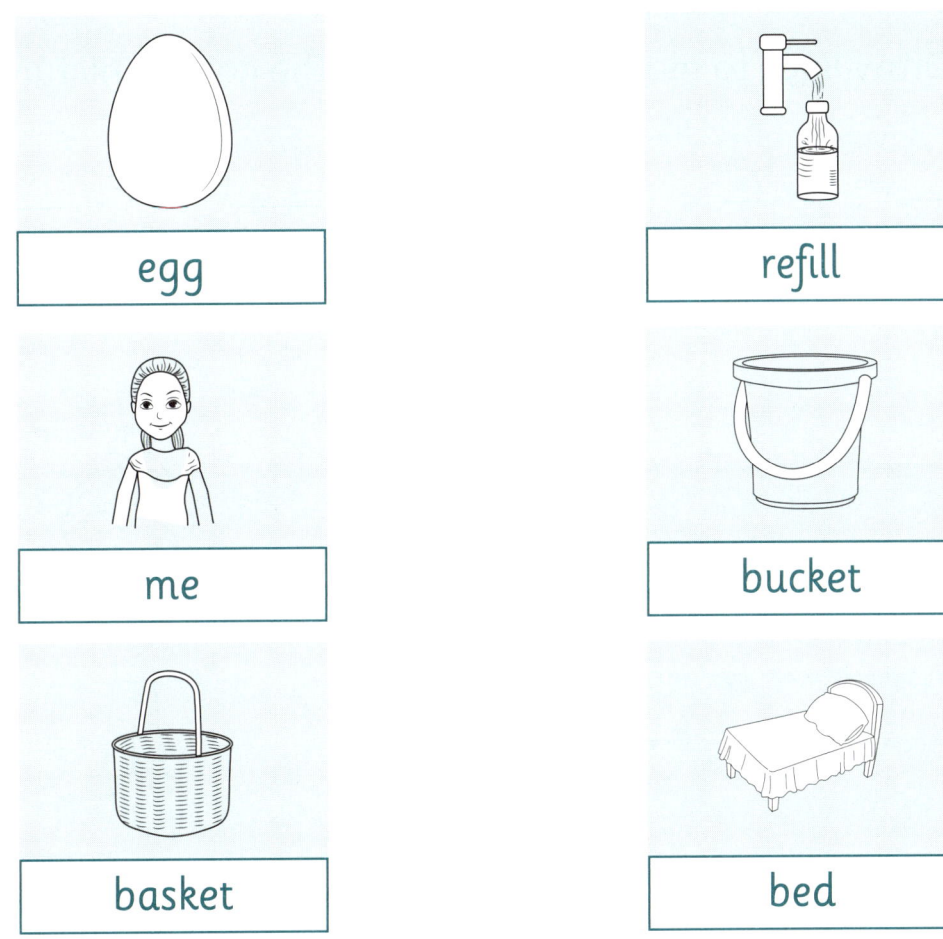

egg

refill

me

bucket

basket

bed

Read and trace the words.

want   what
we   begin

Choose the correct words to finish the sentences.

W_____ do you w_____ to do first?
Shall w_____ b_____?

Template 2

We can say letter **i** in different ways so it sounds like: short '**i**' in **tick** or '**ie**' in **pie**.

We can say letter **y** in different ways so it sounds like: '**y**' in **yak** or '**ee**' in **baby**.

Say the words. Draw lines to match each word to the correct picture.

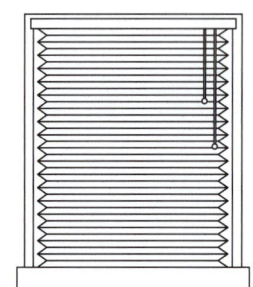

insect
lion
child
blind
pilot
yes
baby
lorry

i and y

Say the words. Choose the correct letter to finish the words.

l _____ on

sunn _____

ch _____ ld

lorr _____

p _____ lot

bab _____

Read and trace the words.

very   suddenly

Choose the correct words to finish the sentence.

_____ the wild lion roared _____ loudly.

Template 4

We can say letter **o** in different ways so it sounds like: 'o' as in **hot**, 'u' as in **colour** or 'oa' as in **most**.

We can say letter **u** in different ways so it sounds like: 'u' as in **hut**, short 'oo' as in **bush**, or 'ue' as in **glue**.

Use the pictures. Say the words. Write one letter in each box.

Write the words in the correct box.

Words with o	Words with u

o and u

Say the words. Choose the correct letters to finish the words.

cl_____thes   o / u

m_____ther   o / u

p_____st   o / u

f_____ll   o / u

Read and trace the words.

over   only   put

some   other

Template 5

We can say letters **ie** in different ways so it sounds like: 'ie' and 'ee'.
We can say letters **ea** in different ways so it sounds like: 'e' and 'ee'.
Underline the words with **ie** or **ea**.

The eagle cleans its feathers with its beak.

It sees some children having a picnic in a field.

The eagle sees some pie.

With a loud shriek, it grabs a piece of pie. The thief!

Write the words in the correct boxes.

Words with ie		Words with ea	
'ie' sound as in tie	'ee' sound as in bee	'e' sound as in bread	'ee' sound as in bead

36

ie and ea

The robot turns mixed-up letters into words. Write the words.

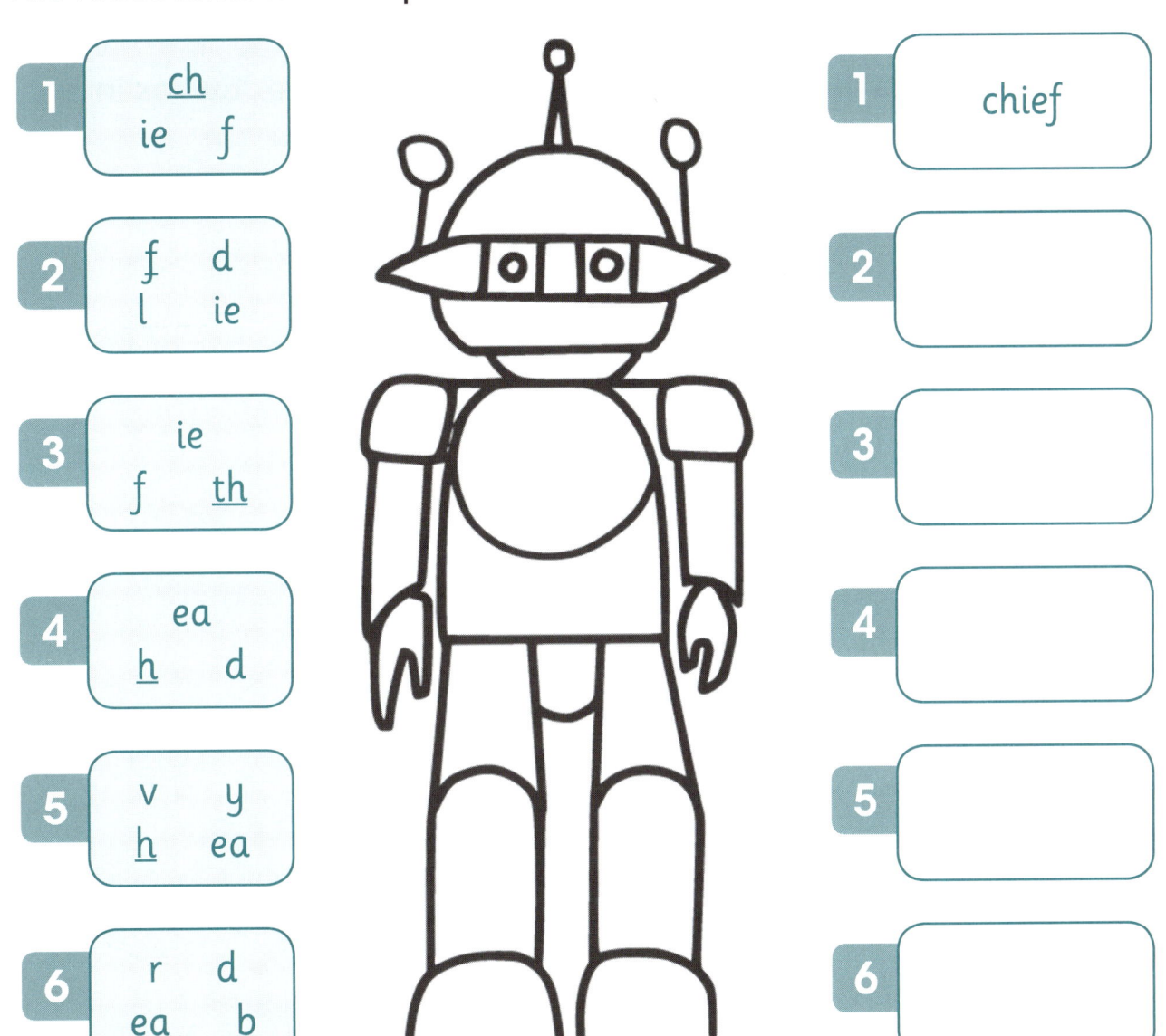

1. ch ie f → chief
2. f d l ie →
3. ie f th →
4. ea h d →
5. v y h ea →
6. r d ea b →

Read and trace the words.

friend   each
really   easy

37

Template 2 and 3

We can say letters **ow** in different ways so they sound like: '**ow**' as in **owl** and '**oa**' as in **elbow**.

We can say letters **ou** in different ways so it sounds like: '**ow**' as in **house** and '**ue**' as in **you**.

Say the words. Draw lines to match each word to the correct picture.

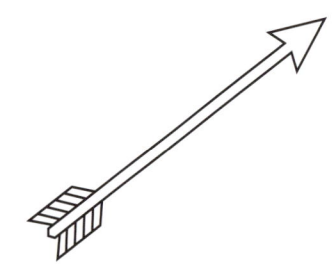

arrow

flower

mouse

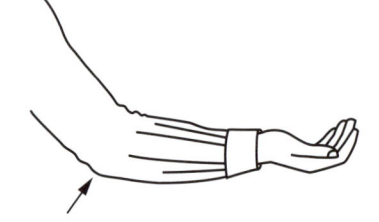

elbow

soup

shoulders

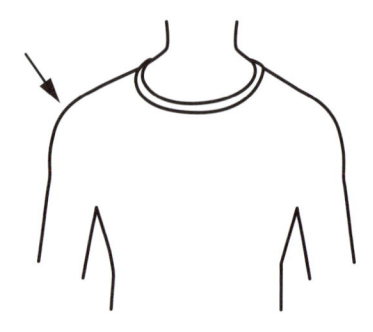

group

house

ow and ou

Read the questions. Write yes or no.

Can you see a shadow?

_____

Can you run about in the playground?

_____

Is she throwing the ball over her shoulder?

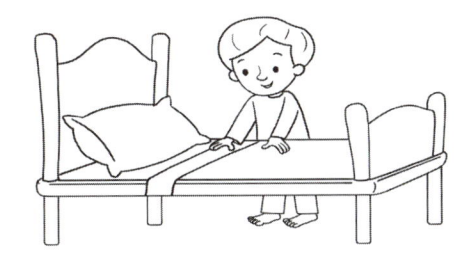

_____

Do you use a pillow when you have a shower?

_____

Template 4

We can say letter **c** in different ways so it sounds like: '**k**' or '**s**'.
We can say letter **g** in different ways so it sounds like: '**g**' and '**j**'.
Use the pictures. Say the words. Write one letter in each box.

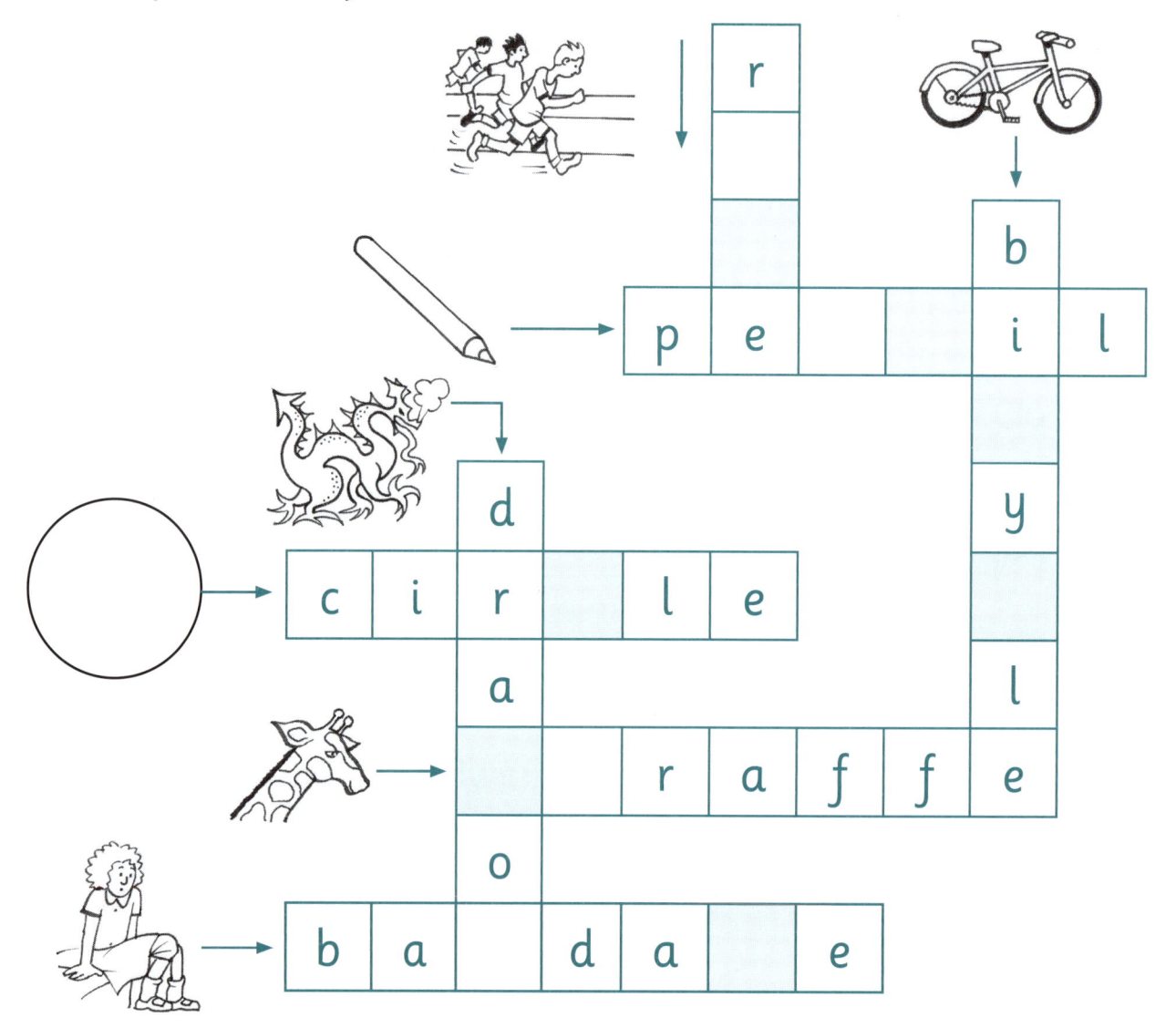

		r				
						b
	p	e			i	l
		d			y	
c	i	r		l	e	
		a				l
			r	a	f	f	e
		o				
b	a		d	a		e

Write the words in the correct boxes.

Words with c		Words with g	
'**k**' sound as in **cat**	'**s**' sound as in **city**	'**g**' sound as in **girl**	'**j**' sound as in **age**

40

c and g

Say the words. Choose the correct letters to finish the words.

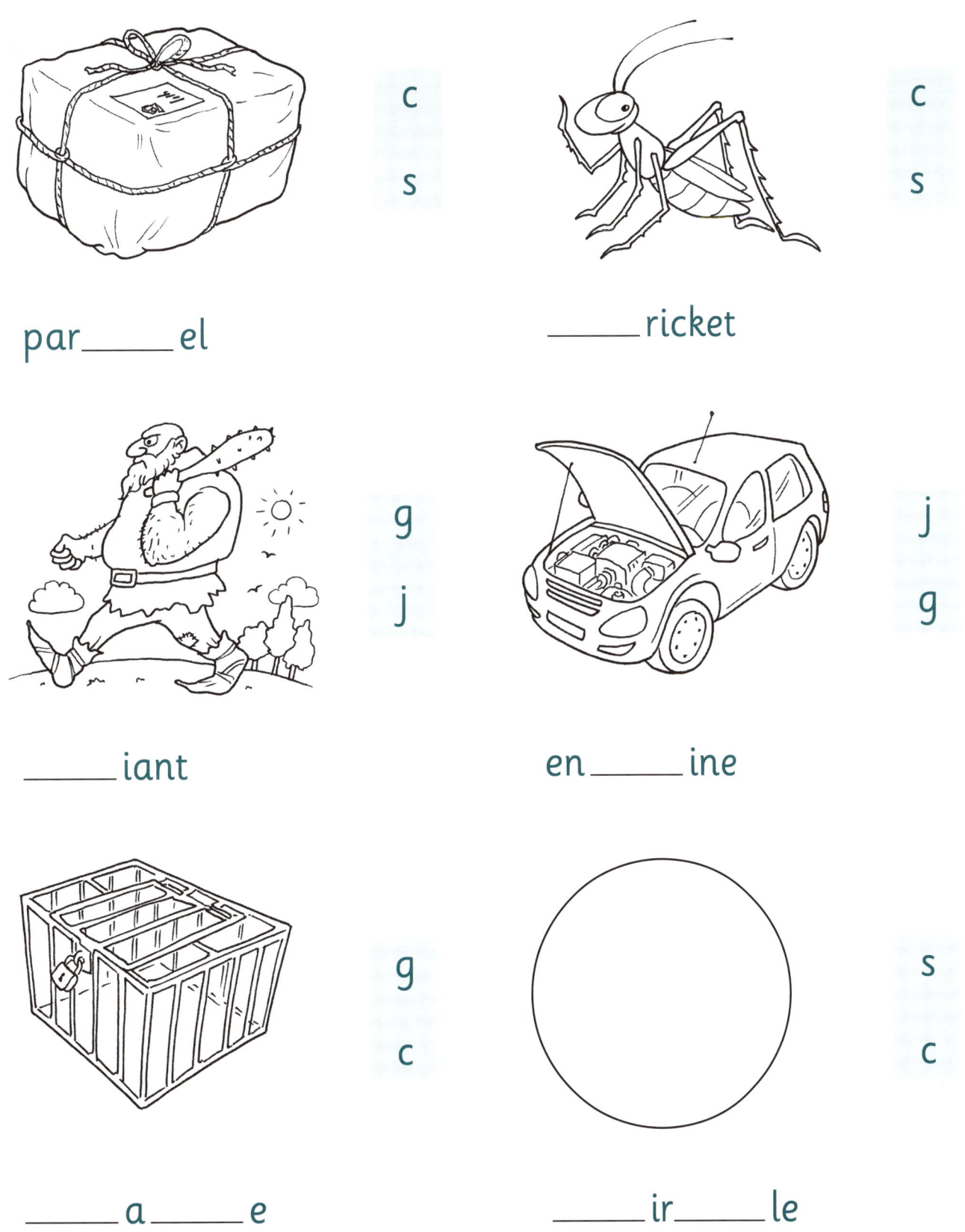

par____el   c / s

____ricket   c / s

____iant   g / j

en____ine   j / g

____a____e   g / c

____ir____le s / c

Template 3

> Look back

Check what you know!

Read the words and draw the pictures.

giraffe	rainbow	gloves	head
lion	pencil	engine	soup
heavy	bull	lorry	circle
dancer	friends	feathers	swan

Look back

Read and trace the words.

even

ever

Read the questions. Write yes or no.

Do you ever dance in the bath?

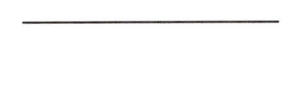

_____

Is five an even number?

_____

Do giraffes ever have feathers?

_____

Do they have an even number of cakes?

_____

Template 1

We can say letter **s** in different ways so it sounds like:
'**s**' as in seven or '**z**' as in trees.

Draw lines to join each word to the correct picture.

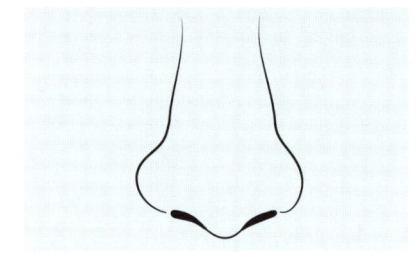

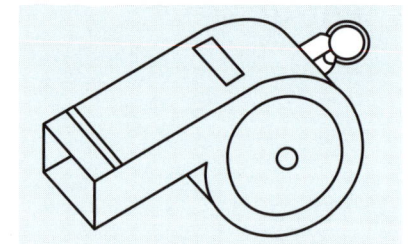

present
nose
castle
cheese
ears
horse
mouse
whistle

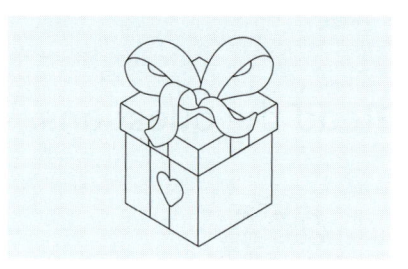

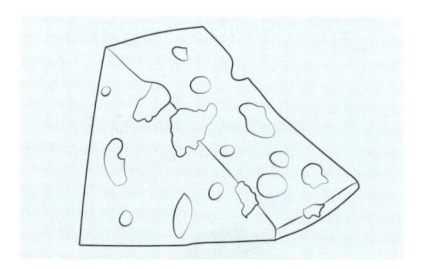

Sort and write the words in the correct boxes.

's' sound as in sister	'z' sound as in visit

's' and 'z'

Say the words. Join the words where letter **s** sounds the same.

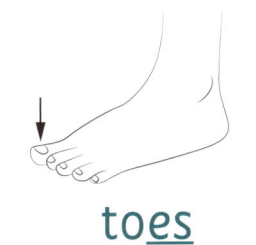

hou<u>se</u>

clot<u>hes</u>

noi<u>se</u>

ca<u>s</u>tle

gla<u>ss</u>

to<u>es</u>

Sound out **p-l-ea-se**

Read and trace the word.

please

Sound out **l-i-st-en**

Read and trace the word.

listen

Read the sentence.

Please listen and I will tell you what we are going to do next.

Template 6 and 5

Read the words and draw the pictures.

Hint: the underlined letters make a 'sh' sound.

| sugar | station | ocean |

Hint: the underlined letters make a 'zh' sound.

| television | treasure | measure |

Hint: the underlined letters make a 'ch' or a 'j' sound.

| picture | bridge | edge |

'sh', 'zh', 'ch', 'j'

Underline the words with 'sh', 'ch', 'j' or 'zh'.

I saw a strange creature on the television.

It was like a mixture of a dragon and a sheep.

I drew a special picture of it having an adventure. It took me ages to draw.

Mum put it in her treasure chest.

Write the words in the correct boxes.

'sh' sound as in station	'ch' sound as in nature	'j' sound as in badge	'zh' sound as in measure

47

Template 4

There are different ways of spelling the sounds 'ai', 'ee', 'ie' and 'oa'. Say the words. Choose the correct letters to finish the words.

ai

a_e

sn____k____

ee

ey

donk____

ee

y

Mumm____

y

ie

cr____

ow

oe

sn____man

ea

ee

sh____p

48

More about: 'ai', 'ee'. 'ie', 'oa'

Use the pictures. Say the words. Write one letter in each box.

Write the words in the correct boxes.

'ai' sound as in play	'ee' sound as in sunny	'ie' sound as in light	'oa' sound as in show

49

Template 6

We can spell the sounds long 'oo', 'or', 'ir' and 'ar' in different ways. Read the words and draw the pictures.

comp<u>u</u>ter	w<u>al</u>k	p<u>a</u>lm tree
<u>Ea</u>rth	f<u>ou</u>r	resc<u>ue</u>
s<u>ear</u>ch	w<u>or</u>m	d<u>au</u>ghter

More about: 'oo', 'or', 'ir', 'ar'

Read the story. Underline the words with the sounds long 'oo' as in blue, 'or' as in draw, 'ir' as in early or 'ar' as in grass.

There are worms in the earth in our garden. If a bird eats half a worm it can grow again.

You have to get up early and search for them. Sometimes the birds eat them.

If you stand as still as a statue, the birds come quite close.

Once a bird caught a worm but then the bird dropped it and flew away.

Write the words in the correct boxes.

long 'oo' sound as in threw	'or' sound as in four	'ir' sound as in urn	'ar' sound as in last

Template 2

Say the words. Draw lines to match each word to the correct picture.

flower
zebra 
colour 
theatre 
camera 
caterpillar 
visitor 
father 

All these words end in the same sound. Draw a circle around the letters that show the last sound in each word.

'er'

Say the words. Choose the correct letters to finish the words:
er, **ar**, **re** or **a**.

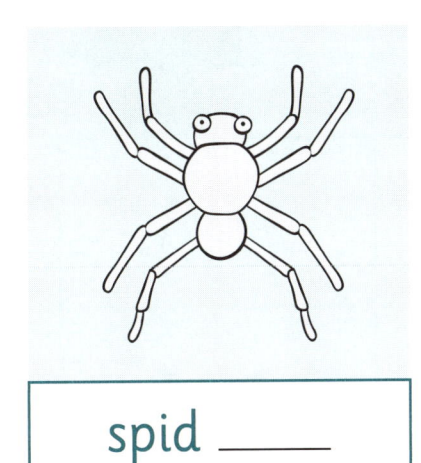

spid _____

sug _____

whisp _____

trous _____ s

fi _____

pand _____

Read and trace the words.

water other

Choose the correct words to finish the sentence.

Please pour some _____ into the _____ cups.

Template 3

> Look back

Check what you know!

Read the words and draw the pictures or look at the pictures and write the words.

	cheese	castle	
treasure	sugar	cushion	station
		honey	
	world		learn

Look back

Read the questions. Write **yes** or **no**.

Did the bird learn to catch a worm?

_____

Is the statue a mixture of an eagle and a lion?

_____

Has the creature escaped from its cage?

_____

Can you measure the size of a planet?

_____

Is strawberry your favourite ice-cream flavour?

_____

Phonics Workbook B

> Teaching phonics using Phonics Workbook B

Cambridge Primary English Phonics Workbooks A and B provide a structured introduction to phonics to underpin the Cambridge Primary English course. The books can also supplement other English courses.

Phonics is an important skill to learn in the early stages of reading and writing. This workbook is intended to be used by learners who already know:

- the sounds represented by all of the letters of the alphabet
- one sound represented by the two letters (digraphs) **sh**, **ch**, **th**, **ai**, **ee**, **ie**, **oa**, **ue**, **ar**, **or**, **ir**, **ou** and **oi** and the three letters (trigraphs) **ear** and **air**
- how to **blend** known letters and digraphs to read an unknown word
- how to **segment** a word into its sounds to spell it.

If your learners are not secure with this, they will benefit from revisiting Phonics Workbook A.

The aim of this workbook is to introduce new combinations of letters that represent sounds, primarily for reading, so that learners are familiar with them. Spelling lessons in future years will help them to learn which choices to make, and this idea is introduced in the Look back pages.

Phonics Workbook B introduces:

- new ways of representing the sounds already known
- the new sound /zh/ as in trea**s**ure
- new ways of pronouncing some familiar letter patterns
- using familiar letter patterns when reading longer words
- the meanings of the words 'vowel' and 'consonant'.

If you are working with learners for whom English is a second language, make sure that the vocabulary used on each page is familiar to them. These workbooks do not use the International Phonetic Alphabet (IPA), which gives symbols instead of letter patterns. For the learners, letter sounds are represented in the workbook in inverted commas.

Letter names and letter sounds

When using this workbook, learners will need to know letter names (for example, **a** = **ai**; **b** = **bee**; **c** = **cee**) as well as their sounds (for example, **b** = **buh**; **f** = **fff**; **g** = **guh**). When you help a learner to hear the sounds in a word for reading or spelling, say the sounds you hear – for example, l-igh-t = light.

Encourage them to continue to use 'phonic fingers' to show the sounds in a word. They should hold up one finger to represent each sound, then sweep the index finger of their other hand across all of the fingers that are held up and say the whole word – for example, l-igh-t = **light**.

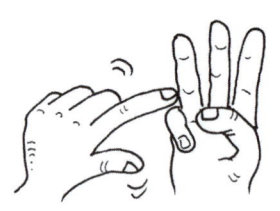

Using this workbook

Continuing the approach in Phonics Workbook A, the activities in Phonics Workbook B are intended to follow an introductory session that you do with the learners using objects, pictures and cards showing letters and letter patterns that they can manipulate. You will find it useful to have sets of cards showing all familiar letters (single, double, triple) for sounds learned so far. As new letter combinations for known sounds are introduced, make cards for them too. A split digraph is when two letters (for example, **a** and **e**) make a sound together but are split within a word (for example, m**a**k**e**). When introducing split digraphs, leave a space on the card that is wide enough to insert other single-letter cards.

Encourage the learners to use the cards:

- in practical activities, placing cards next to pictures or objects
- in sorting activities, where you ask the learners to make sets of pictures, objects and letter patterns that all have the same sound
- to create new words by combining cards; this allows learners to reinforce their understanding of the sounds in words and the sounds represented by each of the new letter patterns as flashcards, so that when you show them a sequence of letters (for example, **igh**) they respond with the sound it represents
- in games. Play snap and memory games using sets of the cards. Encourage the learners to recognise pairs of letter patterns that represent the same sound (for example, **ie** and **igh**).

Introducing new ways of representing letter sounds

Phonics is best presented as a multisensory activity to support learners to remember letter formation, letter names and associated sounds. The activities on pages 10–29 and pages 44–55 are intended to build on learners' existing knowledge about how to represent a letter sound. Making choices about which letter pattern to use is the beginning of learning how to spell.

When introducing new letter combinations:

- always start from what is already known, so begin by revising the familiar letter combinations that represent the target sound
- start working orally, using pictures, objects and letter-pattern cards, saying the sounds in words before showing the learners the new letter pattern; this helps them to associate the letter patterns with representative pictures and objects
- Encourage learners to form the new letter combinations in sand, salt or flour, in the air, and on whiteboards and paper; if they can, encourage learners to join the letters so that they have a fluent knowledge of what the letter pattern looks like, the sounds it represents and the feel of writing it to establish fine motor skills

Before the learners start each activity in the workbook, ensure that they know all the words, that they have already linked each word with the letter pattern needed to write it and that they fully understand what they need to do.

Introducing new ways of pronouncing known letter patterns

English is a complex language to read and spell; not only are there lots of ways of representing each sound, but there is often a variety of ways to pronounce the letter patterns. The activities on pages 30–43 introduce some of these.

As before:

- always start from what is already known, so begin by revising the familiar pronunciations of the letter or letter pattern
- start working orally, using pictures, objects and letter pattern cards, and saying the sounds in words. Ask learners to sort pictures according to the vowel sounds. Then introduce the written forms of the words and discuss the different sounds made by the same letter or letter pattern.

Common words

Some sessions end with the introduction of associated words that need to be learned but do not always follow phonic rules. Encourage the learners to try a 'phonics first' approach to tackling these words for reading and spelling. They should apply what they know and try to work out the word. As they do so, they will begin to see where they need to tweak certain letters or sounds.

Assessment

This workbook is cumulative, allowing learners to practise what they have previously learned. Use observations of the learners' progress to identify when a learner needs support and, if necessary, revise activities, both in the workbook and by using your own resources.

In addition, there are **Look back** pages at the end of every section. Use these to assess and monitor learning. Before you progress beyond a **Look back** page, make sure that each learner can read all of the words and short texts.

Phonics Workbook B

Teaching using template 1

Template 1 is used as follows:

Page numbers	Phonics focus	Words to look out for
12–13	ee, ea and e	meal, reading, cheese, tree, feet, bee, three, leaf, sea, bean, beak
22–23	ow, ou, oy, oi	owl, mouse, cloud, shout boy, coin, soil, enjoy
31	Pronouncing e	egg, bed; me, refill; basket, bucket
44–45	s and z	castle, whistle, horse, mouse nose, ears, present, cheese

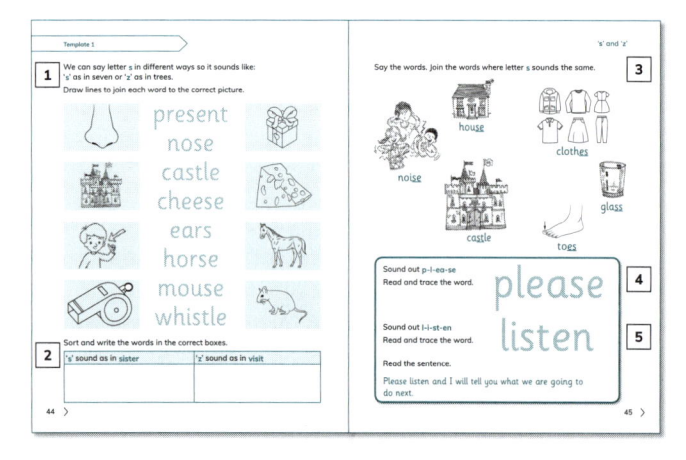

Teaching sequence

1. Read the instruction aloud to the learners. This is primarily a listening activity, not a writing activity. Together, search for words that match the pattern given. Learners may identify words in addition to those shown above, or they may not find them all. Once you have identified words together, tell the learners to ring or label them as requested in the instruction. If there are words, as shown here, ask learners to read – or in some cases complete – the words, and join them to an appropriate part of the picture.

2. Read the instruction aloud to the learners. Before they start to draw or write, ask them to suggest a list of words that might be appropriate.

3. Read the instruction aloud to the learners. Again, this is a listening activity where they are asked to identify words according to their sounds. Ask learners to say the words aloud as they do the activity. It may be easier for them to work in pairs for this part of the activity.

4. This panel is used to introduce common, often tricky words that cannot be read using phonics alone. Read the word aloud for the learners. Each time they finish writing the word over the letters shown, ask them to say the word aloud.

5. Read the sentence aloud to the learners. Ask them to follow with their fingers, pointing to each word as you read it aloud. Remind the learners of the target word. Ask them to re-read the sentence with you, pointing to each word as they do so. Finally, ask learners to re-read the sentence themselves, ringing the target words when they see them.

Teaching using Phonics Workbook B

Teaching using template 2

Template 2 is used as follows:

Page numbers	Phonics focus	Words to look out for
8–9	oi, ow, ar, or, ir and er	shark, shirt, owl, star, coin, arm, skirt, car, horn
20–21	ar, ir, ur, or, aw, ore	goal, snore, shark, hurt, saw, fork, your, are, more
30	Pronouncing a	apple, ant; path, plant; apron, baby; swan, watch
32–33	Pronouncing i and y	lion, sunny, child, lorry, pilot, baby suddenly, very
38	Pronouncing ow and ou	ow arrow, flower, elbow ou mouse, soup, shoulders, group, house
52–53	'er': fath<u>er</u>, zeb<u>ra</u>, visit<u>or</u>	spider, sugar, whisper, trousers, fire, panda

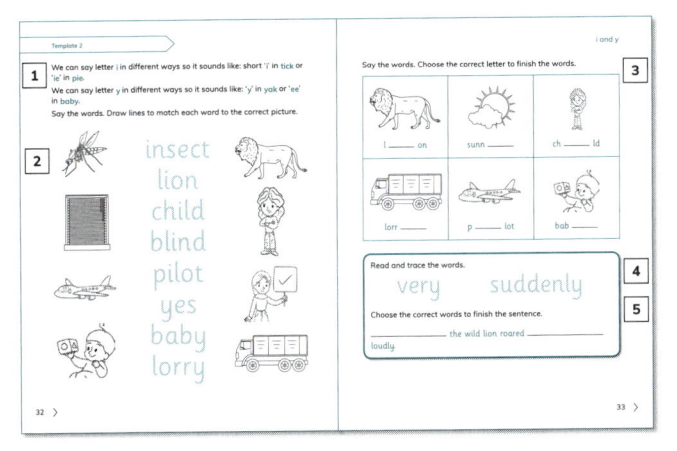

Teaching sequence

1 Read the instruction aloud to the learners. Ask them to read the words in the central box aloud. Check that the vocabulary is familiar. Once the learners know the words, they should trace over them in this panel.

2 Identify the pictures. Make sure that the learners are familiar with the words. Once they have joined each word to its picture, ask them to sound out and copy the word in the box under each picture.

3 Read the instruction aloud to the learners. Together, name all of the pictures. Ask the earners to finish writing the words on the page. Suggest that they use the letter patterns from the previous page. Ask learners to then blend the sounds right through the word to check their spelling.

4 This panel is used to introduce common, often tricky words that cannot be read using phonics alone. Read the words aloud for the learners. They should copy over the word, then write it independently along the line.

5 Read the sentence aloud to the learners. When you reach a blank, ask them which of the words in the box they would use to fill it. Let the learners work independently to fill the gaps.

Phonics Workbook B

Teaching using template 3

Template 3 is used as follows:

Page numbers	Phonics focus	Words to look out for
7	**ai, ee, ie, oa**, long **oo** and short **oo**	sheep, foot, boot, food, sail, boat
28–29	Look back	cake, tray, tree, leaf, bike, fly, light, pie, toe, bone, blow, coat, boot, glue, flute, foot, bird, cow, cloud, deer
39	ow and ou	Words given
42–43	Look back	Words given
54–55	Look back	Words given

Teaching sequence

1. Sometimes the learners see pictures and have to write words here. On other pages, they are given words and are asked to draw the pictures. Read the instruction aloud to the learners. Make sure the words are familiar. Assess their learning and progress, and identify any sounds or letter patterns that cause confusion.

2. This panel is not always present. It is used to introduce common, often tricky words that cannot be read using phonics alone. Read the word aloud for the learners. Ask them to copy over the letters, then to write the word independently. Each time they finish writing the word over the letters shown, ask the learners to say the word aloud.

3. Read the instruction aloud to the learners. Ask them to look at each of the pictures, then to read each question aloud. The questions refer to the pictures. Learners should write 'yes' or 'no' after the question mark to answer the questions.

Teaching using Phonics Workbook B

Teaching using template 4

Template 4 is used as follows:

Page numbers	Phonics focus	Words to look out for
5	**sh, th, ch, ng** and **nk**	
6	**ai, ee, ie, oa,** long **oo** and short **oo**	paint, sheep, tie, soap, foot, boot
16–17	**oa, o_e, ow** and **oe**	toad, goal, goat, bone, stone, toe, rainbow coat, window
26–27	**f, ff, ph, w, wh**	dolphin, twins, phone, wheel, cliff, coffee, window, whale, photograph, sniff
34–35	**o** hot, colour, most **u** hut, bush, glue	piano, cola, octopus, glove pull, bull, superman
40–41	**c** cat, city **g** girl, giraffe	circle ('k' and 's'), bicycle ('k' and 's'), race, pencil, dragon, giraffe, bandage
48–49	ai ee ie oa	crayon seat, happy, monkey night throw, window

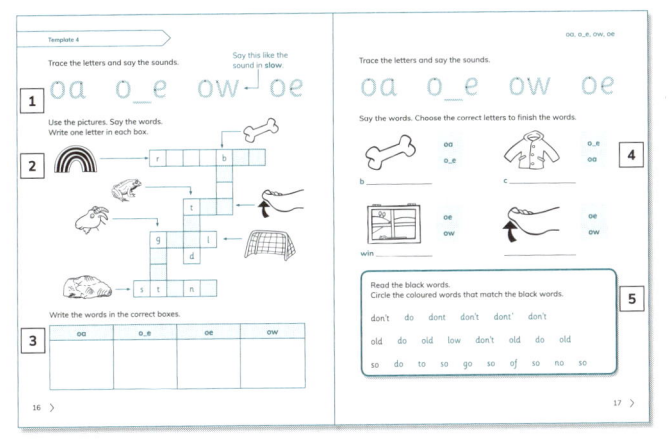

Teaching sequence

1. This panel is not always present. Say the sounds aloud and ask learners to repeat them with you. Learners can then trace the letter patterns on the page. Note that on page 16 the 'ow' represents the sound in 'slow' rather than in 'how'.
2. Read the instruction aloud to the learners. Ask them to identify the pictures. Ask the learners to work out what the missing letters are in each word. One letter should go in each box. The letters in tinted boxes combine to make one sound (digraphs). Tell them to complete the page independently.
3. Read the instruction aloud to the learners. This is a sorting activity that asks the learners to separate the words according to sounds in the words.
4. Read the instruction aloud to the learners. Ask them to identify the pictures. Explain that they have to write letters to finish the words. Show them the boxes and tell them that they must choose from one of the choices in the box. Model completing the first word together, then leave the learners to finish the task independently. Ask learners to blend the sounds right through the word to check their spelling.
5. This panel is not always present. It is used to introduce common, often tricky words that cannot be read using phonics alone. Read the instruction aloud to the learners. Help them to read the words in the box. They should trace over each word, then write the words independently underneath.

Phonics Workbook B

Teaching using template 5

Template 5 is used as follows:

Page numbers	Phonics focus	Words to look out for
10–11	ai, a_e and ay	Layla, came, play, day, came, play, games, race, sailing, rain, made cakes, play, day. bake, tray, tale, train, came, tail
18–19	Long oo, ue, u_e and ew Short oo and u	good, put, new, blue, boots, grew, flew, moon, tunes, flute, bush, stood, shook, soon, took
36–37	ie tie, field ea bead, bread	pie, field, shriek, piece, thief feathers, eagle, cleans, beak
47	sh and zh ch and j	(sh) sheep, special (ch), creature, mixture, picture, adventure, chest (j), strange, ages (zh), television, treasure

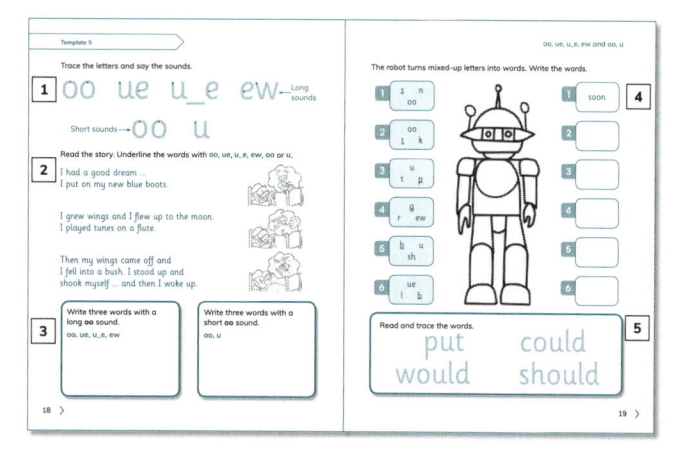

Teaching sequence

1. This panel is not always present. Say the sounds aloud and ask the learners to repeat them with you. They can then trace the letter patterns on the page.
2. Introduce this short story. Make sure the learners know that they will need to read it aloud. They should be able to read all of the words in the story. Once they have read the story, the learners should identify and mark words as indicated.
3. Read the instruction aloud to the learners. This is a sorting activity, where they are asked to think about the sounds and letter patterns in the words they have marked.
4. Read the instruction aloud to the learners. Explain that the robot is a word-making robot – you feed it letters and it makes them into words. The learners' task is to predict which word the robot will make. The first sound in the word is often underlined. Show the learners that each box of letters is numbered. They need to write their answer in the empty box with the same number on the opposite side of the sheet. Model working through the first of the words and show the learners where the answer is written. Give them time to work through the rest of the page independently. Ask learners to blend the sounds right through the word to check their spelling.
5. This panel is used to introduce common, often tricky words that cannot be read using phonics alone. Read the words aloud for the learners. Ask them to trace them on the page, then to write the words independently.

Teaching using Phonics Workbook B

Teaching using template 6

Template 6 is used as follows:

Page numbers	Phonics focus	Words to look out for
4	sh, th, ch, ng and nk	ship, chin, fish, sink, king, swing
14–15	ie, i_e, igh and y	tie, bike, ride, night, light, fly
24–25	air, are, ear, eer	chair, stare, hair, ear, deer, cheer, dear, there, deer, their
46	sh and zh ch and j	Words given
50–51	long oo, including (y)oo, or, ir and ar	('oo') you, statue, flew; ('or') for; ('ir') worms, earth, bird, early, search; ('ar') are, garden, half

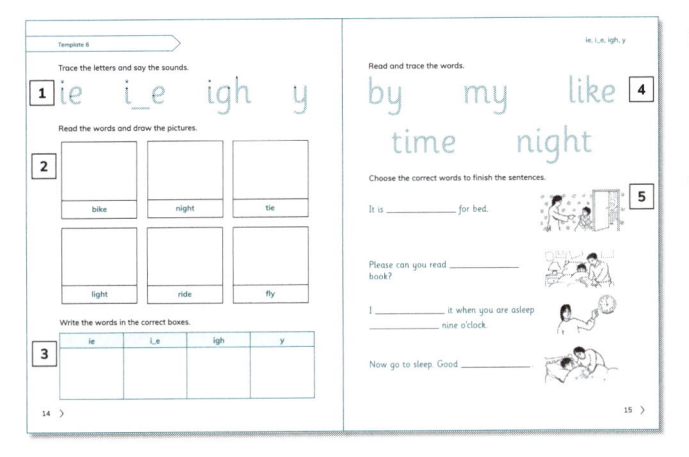

Teaching sequence

1. This panel is not always present. Say the sounds aloud and ask the learners to repeat them with you. They should then trace the letters inside the outlines.
2. Read the instruction aloud to the learners. Ask them to identify the pictures. Encourage them to tell you the sounds in each word as they use 'phonic fingers' to show each sound. Support the learners as they use their phonics fingers to help them to think about each sound as they write it to spell the words.
3. This panel is not always present. Read the instruction aloud to the learners. Ask them to sort the words they have written in the table according to the sound in the words.
4. This panel is not always present. It is used to introduce common, often tricky words that cannot be read using phonics alone. Read the words aloud to the learners and talk about the letters in them. Ask them to write and say the words. Warn them that they will need to remember the words for the reading activity.
5. Read the instruction aloud to the learners. Tell them to read each sentence and look at the picture. In some versions of the template, learners should use the common words to complete the sentences. In other versions of the template, there are no gaps but learners are asked to identify words with particular sounds, which they are then asked to sort in a table at the foot of the page. Once you have completed the first sentence together, allow the learners to work independently to complete the activity.

Phonics Workbook B

Pronunciation guide

These workbooks do not use the International Phonetic Alphabet (IPA), which gives symbols instead of letter patterns. Use this chart to help guide pronunciation using the word examples provided. For example, the sound 'ai' may be spelt as ai, a-e, ay and the letters ow may be pronounced differently in words 'show' and 'how'.

Page	Letters and sounds	Example words with associated tricky words (common exception words) in brackets
10–11	ai, a_e, ay	again, made, always (came, made, make, today, always)
12–13	ee, ea, e	seen, these, sea (please, people)
14–15	ie, i_e, igh, y	tie, time, high, fly (like, time, my, by, might)
16–17	oa, o_e, ow, oe	boat, more, slow, toe, so (don't, so, old)
18–19	long oo, ue, u_e, ew, short oo, u	zoom, tune, blue, flew, super, computer book, put, could (would, should)
20–21	ar, ir, ur or, aw, ore	shark, girl, burn (are) sport, saw, store (your, saw, more)
22–23	ow, ou oi, oy	owl, shout (about) coin, boy
24–25	air, are, ear eer	chair, stare, wear deer, near (there, their)
26–27	f, ff, ph w, wh	fish, cliff, dolphin went, whale (where, when)
30–31	a e	apple, baby, father, swan (ask, after, what, want) egg, eleven, basket
32–33	i y	insect, find yes (very, suddenly)
34–35	o u	octopus, piano, mother (over, other, only, some, one) under, bull, super
36–37	ie ea	lie, field (friend) eagle, head (really, each, easy)
38–39	ow ou	now, show mouse, soup, shoulder
40–41	c g	cat, city girl, giraffe
44–45	s	sister, whistle, hiss, (listen) nose, (please)
46–47	'sh' 'zh' 'ch' 'j'	ship, sugar, station, ocean vision, measure children, picture jump, bridge
52–53	'er'	flower, colour, zebra, visitor, theatre (water, other)